4

Contents

4242-48
ISBN: 0-8054-4248-0

Dewey Decimal Classification: J220.92
Subject heading: WOMEN IN THE BIBLE

Printed in the United States of America.

Women in the Bible
Helpful Friends

JUDY LATHAM • ILLUSTRATED BY **PAUL KARCH**

BROADMAN PRESS
Nashville, Tennessee

Deborah: Friend of a Nation

After Joshua died, the people of Israel forgot God. They broke his laws. They worshiped idols.

This made God angry. He let an evil, harsh man, Jabin, control the land. The caravans stopped coming through Israel. People were afraid to travel on the main roads and hid in their homes. The people of Israel knew they had sinned. They begged God to help them.

God heard his people's prayers. He chose Deborah to be a judge and to help the people. Deborah was a wise and gentle woman. Every day she sat under a palm tree and talked with the people. The people trusted Deborah. She was God's leader.

One day Deborah sent for her friend Barak. He came and sat with her under the palm tree.

"Barak," said Deborah, "The Lord is ready to deliver Israel from Jabin. I want you to help me. I have a plan. But first, we must get an army of ten thousand men. Then we will fight Jabin's army and its leader, Sisera."

"But, Deborah, that is not enough men to fight Sisera," argued Barak.

"Yes, Barak, it is enough," Deborah said. "God will help us. I will lure Sisera's army into the river valley. Then you will charge them from the mountain."

"That is a good plan," Barak agreed. "I will fight against Sisera, but only if you go with me."

Deborah nodded her head and smiled, "I'll go with you, my friend. God will go with us both."

Barak and Deborah traveled over the land getting soldiers to fight against Sisera. Everywhere they went, Deborah said to the people, "God will help our land! But we must fight. Sisera and his army must be defeated. Come, join our army! Bring your weapons! God will help us!"

Soon ten thousand men were camped around the mountain. Some had wooden shields covered with leather. Some carried bows and arrows. Most had bronze or copper daggers. Some had only slings and rocks. But they all believed in Deborah. They knew God would help them. The soldiers were ready to fight.

Meanwhile, Sisera's spies came to him with a message, "Deborah and Barak are camped on Mount Tabor with ten thousand soldiers."

"Ha!" laughed Sisera. "Ten thousand soldiers are not enough to fight me. I have ten times that many men in my army. I have trained soldiers who ride in chariots and fight with iron spears. Deborah and Barak have only shepherds and farmers with nothing but slings and leather shields. This will be an easy battle."

Deborah's army and Sisera's army began moving into the river valley. Barak's army remained hidden on the mountain.

While the men prepared for battle Deborah prayed, "Give us a victory, O, God. Deliver us from our enemy."

Barak stood on the lookout point. He saw Sisera's army getting closer and closer to Deborah's army. Then Barak saw Deborah raise her sword. This was the signal he was waiting for. Barak shouted, "Charge! The men of Israel will defeat the army of Sisera!"

Barak's men charged down the side of
the mountain. They battled Sisera's army
to the river's edge.

Suddenly, a hard rain began to fall. As it
fell the river banks overflowed. The
ground became muddy. The wheels of
Sisera's mighty chariots stuck in the mud.
The river began to flood. Barak and his
men backed Sisera's soldiers deeper and
deeper into the rushing water where most
of them drowned.

9

Deborah and Barak and their army thanked God for the victory. Deborah sang a song telling the story of the battle. Deborah and Barak sang the song as a praise hymn to God as they marched home.

The people of Israel obeyed the laws of God while Deborah judged the nation. Deborah was a strong woman who inspired a nation.

Thinkback: List things Deborah did that women don't often do. How did her faith in God help her do them?

What are some things you could do with God's help?

Esther: Friend of the Jews

Years after Deborah lived the people of Israel forgot God again. This time God let a foreign king conquer the land. This king took many of the Jews to live in his country.

Mordecai was one of these people. He and his family settled in the city of Susa. One member of Mordecai's family was a cousin, Esther.

One day soldiers from the king's palace came to Mordecai's house. They said, "Mordecai, your cousin must come with us. She and other beautiful women have been chosen to live at the king's palace. He will select one to be his queen."

Before Esther left, Mordecai warned

her, "Esther, tell no one you are a Jew. If people know you are a Jew, they might hurt you. Be brave. God will guide you."

When it was Esther's turn to go to the king, she was ready. The king said, "Esther, you are the most beautiful woman

12

in my country. You will be my queen."

At this time a proud and selfish man named Haman was the king's prime minister. Because he was so proud, he ordered everyone to bow to him. But Mordecai refused to bow because he believed in God. This made Haman angry. He wanted to kill Mordecai and all the Jews.

Haman said to the king, "I have a plan to bring money to our treasury. It will also rid our country of dangerous people. I will give you 375 tons of silver if you will let me kill all the Jews in our country. When they are dead, I will take their money and land for our treasury."

"Do what you want," the king told Haman. "The money and the people are yours."

Haman was excited. He wrote a letter that was carried by the king's soldiers all over the country. The letter said that all Jews were to die on the thirteenth of the month Adar.

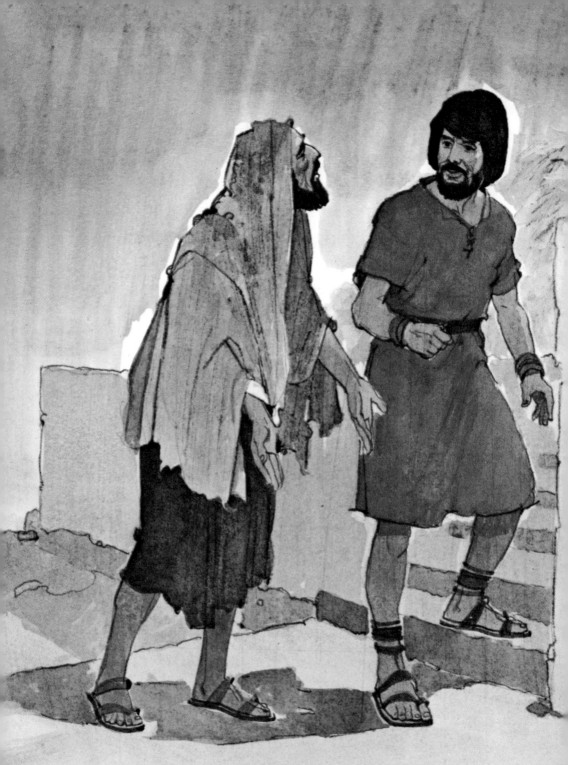

14

All the Jews were sad. Mordecai dressed
in rags and covered his head with ashes.
He cried as he walked to the palace where
he worked. He asked one of Esther's
servants to take her a message. He said,
"Tell Esther to go to the king and beg for
the lives of her people."

Esther heard the message and was
upset. She sent back this message,
"Mordecai, I cannot go to the king unless
he sends for me. If I do, I could be put to
death."

Mordecai was troubled. Esther was the
Jews' only hope. He sent another message:
"Don't think you will escape death. You
will be killed because you are a Jew also.
Perhaps God let you be queen at this time
so that you could save the Jews."

15

Esther thought about her cousin's message. She sent him this answer: "Mordecai, call a meeting of all the Jews in the city. Fast and pray for three days and nights. I will do the same. Then I will go before my king. If I die, then I die."

Three days later Esther dressed in her most beautiful gown and walked into the part of the palace where the king lived. Esther was afraid, but she knew God would be with her.

The king saw Esther coming. He thought to himself: "I did not send for her. I do not know why she is coming, but I am glad to see her." Then he held out his scepter to her.

Esther sighed with relief. This was the signal that she could speak and would not be put to death. She asked the king: "If you would be so kind, dear King, bring Haman and be my guest at a banquet tomorrow." The king agreed.

The next evening everyone enjoyed the banquet. Once again Esther asked the king, "Dear King, if it please you bring Haman to another banquet tomorrow." Again, the king agreed.

As Haman walked home from the banquet he thought about his good luck. "I'm a lucky man," he thought. "The king and queen like me. I am rich and powerful. Next month I'll be rid

of all the Jews."

Just then Haman saw Mordecai. He
forgot all his good luck. Haman could only
think about one Jew who would not bow
before him.

Haman went home and talked to his
family. Then he called for workmen. He
said, "Build me a gallows because
tomorrow I will see that Mordecai hangs."

The next day after the second banquet Queen Esther bowed before the king. She said, "Your majesty, if it please you, let my people, the Jews, live. An evil man is plotting to kill us. Please don't let this happen!"

The king was horrified. He had forgotten about Haman's plan. "Who is planning this awful thing?" he asked. Esther pointed her finger at Haman and said, "He is!"

The king was very angry. He ordered that Haman be killed. One of the soldiers told the king about the gallows Haman had built for Mordecai. The king shouted, "Take him away. Hang him on his own gallows!"

Because of Esther's bravery many lives were saved. Esther was a brave woman who saved her people.

Thinkback: Esther used her position as queen to save her people. Could she have done anything else? Why do you think she decided to do it?

Jewish people today honor Esther for what she did. Talk to a Jewish friend about the Festival of Purim.

Mary and Martha: Friends of Jesus

Everyone in town knew Jesus was coming. Martha was always busy. But when Jesus was due for a visit, she was extra busy. For days Martha had been sweeping and scrubbing her house. Each day she had gathered fruits and vegetables to ripen.

Her oven didn't cool for days as
she baked bread and cakes for her guests.
Martha wanted everything to be
perfect for Jesus.

Her sister Mary was also happy about
Jesus' visit. As soon as she knew Jesus was
coming, Mary climbed
the hill behind her
house to her secret
place.

It was a small

cave in the hillside where she could rest and think. Mary wanted to think about Jesus and his former visit. She thought about the stories Jesus had told and the questions he had answered. Mary liked to talk with Jesus because he took time to listen and answer her questions.

Finally, Jesus had come. Mary and Martha welcomed Jesus to their home. Martha hurried to the kitchen to fix a meal, but Mary stayed near Jesus.

Martha worked quickly. She looked around to give Mary a bowl of fruit to carry to the table, but Mary wasn't there. Martha became angry, "What am I going to do with her. She is never around when I need her."

Martha looked into the room where Jesus was resting and saw Mary. Martha called out, "Master, don't you see how busy I am trying to get food for everyone? Tell Mary to come and help me."

Jesus said, "Martha, Martha, don't worry about feeding us. Calm down. We're fine now. Mary is doing what you should be doing. Come sit here and rest." Martha wiped her hands, put down her bowl, and sat down. She was really glad for a chance to visit with Jesus.

Jesus understood and loved Martha. He knew she was showing her love when she cooked and cleaned and tended to her household chores. Jesus also understood and loved Mary. He knew she was showing her love when she listened eagerly to what he said.

26

When Lazarus became sick, Mary and Martha thought about Jesus. "If Jesus can heal others," they thought, "surely he could heal Lazarus."

But Jesus couldn't come to Bethany right away. When he did come, Lazarus was dead. Jesus was sad because he loved Lazarus.

Jesus told Mary and Martha: "Don't cry anymore. If you believe in me, then believe your brother will live again."

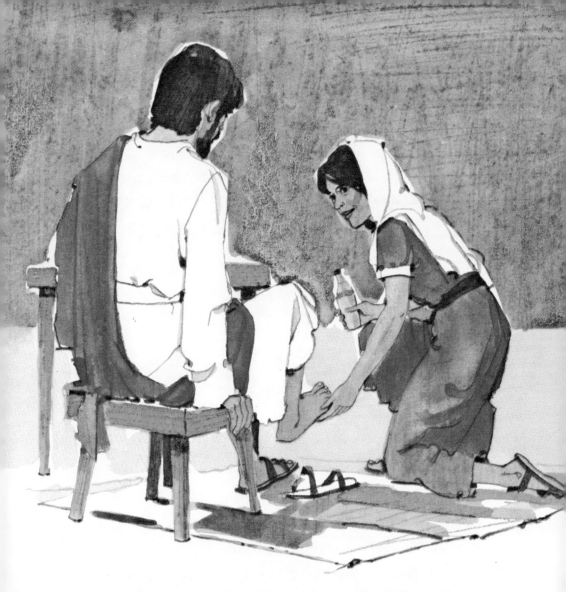

Jesus went to the tomb where Lazarus was buried. He called in a loud voice, "Lazarus, come out!" Lazarus came from the tomb. His sisters were overjoyed. They welcomed Jesus and their friends to their home to celebrate.

Every time Jesus came to Bethany he found comfort and love. Just before the crucifixion he returned to Bethany. Martha prepared a special meal for him.

Jesus wanted his friends to understand what was going to happen to him. He began to talk about his death and resurrection.

Mary understood what Jesus was saying. She knew he was going to suffer. She wanted him to know how much she loved him.

Mary went to her room and got a bottle of expensive oil. Before anyone knew what she was doing, Mary poured the oil on Jesus' feet. Then she took down her hair and dried his feet. Jesus looked into Mary's eyes and said: "Thank you, Mary, for showing how much you love me. I will always remember this."

Many people loved Jesus while he was on earth. Mary and Martha loved Jesus, each in a different way. Martha was an active woman who tended to details. Mary was a thoughtful woman who listened and learned.

Thinkback: Jesus felt good about being at Mary and Martha's house. What are some things you can do to help people feel good about being in your home?

Dorcas: Friend of the Widows

After Jesus returned to heaven, people who believed in him were persecuted. They began leaving Jerusalem to find new homes in safer cities.

Some of the believers went to the seaport town of Joppa. They found jobs, built homes, and started a church. One of the believers was a good woman named Dorcas.

Dorcas lived in a small house near the sea. She was a busy woman. Every day she swept and cleaned her house. Early each morning she got fresh water and baked bread. The rest of the day was spent helping others.

Many poor widows in Joppa had no one to care for them. Dorcas was their friend.

She loved them, and they loved her. She
spent much of her time making clothes for
them. Dorcas also shared her home and
food with the widows.

One afternoon Dorcas began to feel sick. She lay on her couch to rest. Dorcas was hot with fever. The next day she died.

Word spread quickly that Dorcas was dead. Her friends gathered for her burial. They talked about the good things Dorcas had done for others. As they talked, Simeon walked up and asked, "What has happened to Dorcas?"

"She took a fever and died," said one of the widows.

"We are ready to bury her," said another.

"Friends," Simeon said, "Peter is in the next town. We must get a message to him. We must ask him to come and see Dorcas."

"But, Simeon," one of the widows answered, "we are ready to bury her."

"No," answered Simeon, "Keep her body in the upstairs room. Do not bury her. Peter must see her first. I'll go for him."

One of Simeon's friends ran after him, "Simeon, wait! I'll come with you. If we hurry, we can be back by nightfall."

The two men went as fast as they could. Soon they were in Lydda and found Peter.

Simeon said, "Peter, please come to Joppa with us. Our friend Dorcas is dead. She was a good woman. She helped many people. You must see her."

"Dorcas must have been a good woman," Peter said, "for you to have come this far to get me. I will go back with you." The three men returned quickly to Joppa.

When Peter arrived, a crowd had gathered at Dorcas' house. He went to the upstairs room to see Dorcas. Then the widows came to him.

"Peter, see what she made for me," said one, showing Peter a well-made robe.

"Look, Peter," said another, "she just finished this new robe for me."

"Peter, she always shared her food with me," said an older woman.

Peter could see how much the widows loved Dorcas. He asked them to go downstairs.

Peter kneeled by Dorcas' bed and prayed: "Thank you, God, for Dorcas. She was a good woman. She helped others. She believed in Jesus."

Then Peter stood up. He stretched out his hand and said, "Dorcas, get up!" At that moment Dorcas opened her eyes. She looked at Peter's face, took his hand, and sat up.

Peter said: "My name is Peter, I am a disciple of Jesus Christ. God has made you well."

Dorcas bowed her head and said, "Thank you, God, for healing me. Thank you for Peter and for my friends."

Peter took Dorcas downstairs. Her

37

friends began to sing hymns of praise to God. The widows cried for joy. Simeon shook Peter's hand.

Before long everyone in Joppa heard about Dorcas. People came to see her and to listen to her story. Many of them believed in Jesus.

The next day Dorcas cleaned her house and gathered her food. Then she sat down to sew because one of the widows needed a new robe. Dorcas was a good woman who loved the widows.

Thinkback: Dorcas was not a famous or well-known woman, but God let her live again. Why do you think he did this?

ROME

PHILLIPPI

EPHESUS

CORINTH

SYRIA

ANTIOCH

CYPRUS

SAMARIA

DAMASCUS

CANA

CAPERNAUM

NAZARETH

BETHSIADA

LAKE GALILEE

JOPPA

JERUSALEM

LYDDA

BETHANY

SOME NEW TESTAMENT PLACES

39

Lydia: Friend of the Missionaries

When Peter left Joppa he continued
telling people about Jesus. Another
traveling preacher was Paul. One of his
trips took him to the city of Philippi. It was
a rich city with many businesses and many
wealthy people. One of these wealthy
people was a woman named Lydia. She
sold purple cloth, which was very
expensive.

Lydia believed in God. This made her different from most of the people in her city. Each sabbath she closed her shop and went with other women to worship. The women met by the river in a meadow called the prayer place.

One sabbath a young man walked up to
the women and said, "My name is
Timothy. I am a missionary with Paul and
Silas. Is this the prayer place?"

Lydia answered him, "Yes, it is. Would
you join us?"

"Yes," Timothy answered, "but first I
must get the others. We have been looking
for this place."

In a little while Timothy returned with
Paul, Silas, and Luke. The missionaries
told the women their names. Then Paul
said, "We have come to tell you about
Jesus, God's Son, who died for all people."
Everyone listened.

Timothy told the story of Jesus' birth.
Next, Silas told the women about some of
the miracles Jesus had done. Then Paul
preached about Jesus' death and
resurrection. When Paul had finished he
said: "Now you have heard about Jesus. Do
you believe he is your Savior?"

Lydia had listened carefully. She believed in God. She knew God had promised to send a Savior. Now she believed that Jesus was that Savior. Lydia stood and said, "Paul, I accept Jesus as my Savior. Can I be baptized here, today?"

Paul said, "Yes, you can." Paul and Lydia walked into the river. Paul said, "Lydia, my sister in Christ, I baptize you in the name of the Father, the Son, and the Holy Spirit. Amen."

When Lydia came out of the water, she said, "Thank you, God, for sending these men to tell me about Jesus." Then she said to Paul, "Please come home with me. I have a large house and many servants. I have a large business and many workers. I want them to know about Jesus."

Paul and Silas, Timothy and Luke walked home with Lydia. Lydia called her servants and workers together to hear

Paul's message. Many of them believed and were baptized.

That night Lydia sat talking with the missionaries. Her heart was full of love for God. Lydia was glad the missionaries had come to her city. She wanted to find a way to thank them for telling her about Jesus.

Lydia walked to the edge of the balcony and looked out at the city. Then she turned to Paul and said, "Paul, there are many people in my city who need to know about Jesus. Stay at my house. It is large. You will be comfortable. Let me take care of you. That way you will have more time to tell others about Jesus.

Paul smiled and said, "Dear friend, we will be happy to stay with you."

Each day the missionaries preached to the people. Each evening they came back to Lydia's house to eat and rest. Before long there were many new believers.

Lydia took care of Paul and his friends. She also offered her house as the meeting place for a church. Because of Lydia's generosity the church at Philippi was begun. Lydia was a generous woman who shared her wealth.

Thinkback: Jesus said rich people often will not be Christians. Lydia was different. Why? Would it be harder for you to be a Christian if you had lots of money?

Reflections

- Deborah was a friend because she encouraged her nation to do its best. You can encourage others.
- Esther was a friend because she risked her life to save her people. You can stand up for someone who is being hurt or put down.
- Martha was a friend because she helped Jesus feel comfortable in her home. You can welcome others into your home.
- Mary was a friend because she listened to what Jesus said. You can listen to others and learn about them.
- Dorcas was a friend because she helped people who could not help themselves. You can give to others who .are in need.
- Lydia was a friend because she shared her wealth with others. You can share your possessions with others.

47

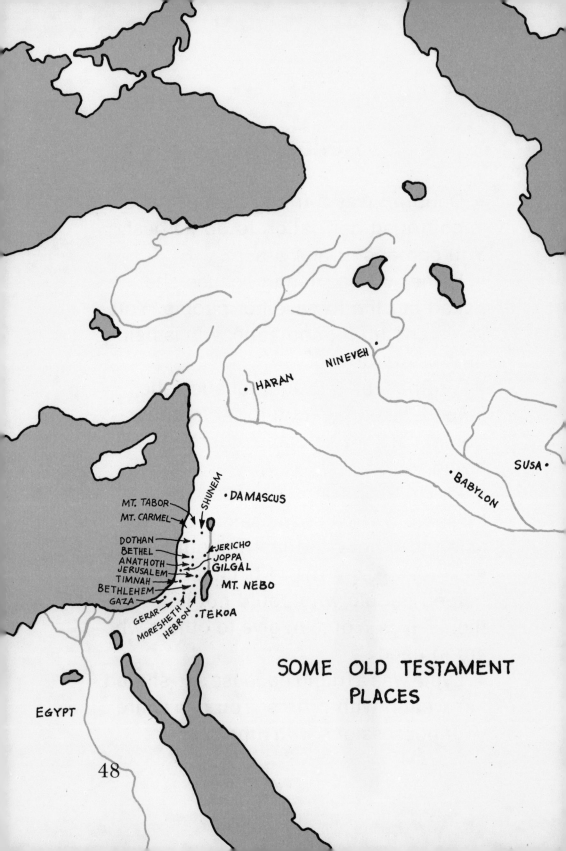

MT. TABOR
MT. CARMEL
SHUNEM
DOTHAN
BETHEL
ANATHOTH
JERUSALEM
TIMNAH
BETHLEHEM
GAZA
GERAR
MORESHETH
HEBRON
TEKOA
• DAMASCUS
•JERICHO
JOPPA
GILGAL
MT. NEBO

HARAN
NINEVEH
BABYLON
SUSA •

EGYPT

SOME OLD TESTAMENT
PLACES

48

429 - 600 - 56323 -202 -696 -3631

CURRICULUM MATERIALS

Date Due

SEP 3 1985			
APR 8 1986			
MAY 2 1 1986			
MAR 1 0 1987			
MAY 1 9 1987			
JAN 2 01			
MAY 07 02			